LET'S FIND OUT! GOOD HEALTH

WHAT ARE CALORIES?

DANIEL E. HARMON

Britannica
Educational Publishing

IN ASSOCIATION WITH

ROSEN
EDUCATIONAL SERVICES

Published in 2019 by Britannica Educational Publishing (a trademark of Encyclopædia Britannica, Inc.) in association with The Rosen Publishing Group, Inc.
29 East 21st Street, New York, NY 10010

Copyright © 2019 The Rosen Publishing Group, Inc. and Encyclopædia Britannica, Inc. Encyclopædia Britannica, Britannica, and the Thistle logo are registered trademarks of Encyclopædia Britannica, Inc. All rights reserved.

Distributed exclusively by Rosen Publishing.
To see additional Britannica Educational Publishing titles, go to rosenpublishing.com.

First Edition

Britannica Educational Publishing
J. E. Luebering: Executive Director, Core Editorial
Mary Rose McCudden: Editor, Britannica Student Encyclopedia

Rosen Publishing
Kathy Kuhtz Campbell: Senior Editor
Nelson Sá: Art Director
Nicole Russo-Duca: Series Designer and Book Layout
Cindy Reiman: Photography Manager
Nicole DiMella: Photo Researcher

Library of Congress Cataloging-in-Publication Data

Names: Harmon, Daniel E., author.
Title: What are calories?/Daniel E. Harmon.
Description: New York: Britannica Educational Publishing, in Association with Rosen Educational Services, 2019. | Series: Let's find out! Good health | Audience: Grades 1–4. | Includes bibliographical references and index.
Identifiers: LCCN 2017047769 | ISBN 9781538303108 (library bound) | ISBN 9781538303115 (pbk.) | ISBN 9781538303122 (6 pack)
Subjects: LCSH: Food—Caloric content—Juvenile literature. | Food—Composition—Juvenile literature. | Energy metabolism—Juvenile literature. | Nutrition—Juvenile literature.
Classification: LCC TX551 .H276 2019 | DDC 613.2/8—dc23
LC record available at https://lccn.loc.gov/2017047769

Manufactured in the United States of America

Photo credits: Cover, back cover, p. 4, interior pages background Dragon Images/Shutterstock.com; p. 5 Lopolo/Shutterstock.com; p. 6 Richard Hutchings/Science Source; p. 7 U.S. Food and Drug Administration; p. 8 Artwork studio BKK/Shutterstock.com; pp. 10, 18 Monkey Business Images/Shutterstock.com; p. 11 Sergey Novikov/Shutterstock.com; p. 12 Imgorthand/E+/Getty Images; p. 13 Png Studio Photography/Shutterstock.com; p. 14 (soda) AlenKadr/Shutterstock.com, (spoon) Sebastian Studio/Shutterstock.com, (milk) addkm/Shutterstock.com, (macaroons) Sathit/Shutterstock.com; p. 15 Robyn Mackenzie/Shutterstock.com; p. 16 fotostorm/E+/Getty Images; p. 17 Paul Burns/Stockbyte/Getty Images; p. 19 Feelkoy/Shutterstock.com; p. 20 margouillat photo/Shutterstock.com; p. 21 kondratya/Shutterstock.com; p. 22 NurPhoto/Getty Images; p. 23 Shannon Fagan/Photodisc/Getty Images; p. 24 VLADIMIR VK/Shutterstock.com; p. 25 George Doyle/Stockbyte/Getty Images; p. 26 Digital Vision/Thinkstock; p. 27 Jovanmandic/iStock/Thinkstock; p. 28 Juice Images/Cultura/Getty Images; p. 29 Ariel Skelley/DigitalVision/Getty Images.

Contents

What Are Calories?	4
Calories in Human Diets	6
How Many Calories Do People Need?	10
Calorie Estimates for Children and Adults	12
Calories Come with Carbohydrates	14
Calories in Sugar	16
Calories in Fats	18
Calories in Proteins	20
Understanding Food Labels	22
"Empty" Calories	24
Problems Caused by Too Many Calories	26
Balancing Calories and Activities	28
Glossary	30
For More Information	31
Index	32

What Are Calories?

Millions of adults carefully count the calories they eat every day. For most, the reason is that they want to lose weight or stay at the same weight. Some people, on the other hand, are thin and weak. They may have lost weight because of an illness. They need to increase their calories to gain weight and build their strength.

Calories can be confusing. People think about calories when they think about their weight, but calories are not a measure of weight. They measure energy. Humans take in energy through food. The human body uses food

A woman uses a computer app to help count the number of calories in a complete serving of a meal.

energy as fuel for its activities. People call this process "burning calories."

Activities that burn calories can be hard work—for example, concentrating on homework or moving heavy boxes. They also can be as easy as breathing and walking. Even sleeping takes a small amount of energy. Each activity burns a certain number of calories.

If people burn more calories than they consume in their food each day, they lose weight. If they burn fewer calories than they consume, their bodies convert the unused calories to fat and store it. That stored fat increases their weight.

Think About It

Instead of measuring the calories people consume and the energy they burn, why don't doctors and dieticians simply keep track of people's weight?

Running and playing sports are good ways to burn calories. Exercise is important for healthy living.

Calories in Human Diets

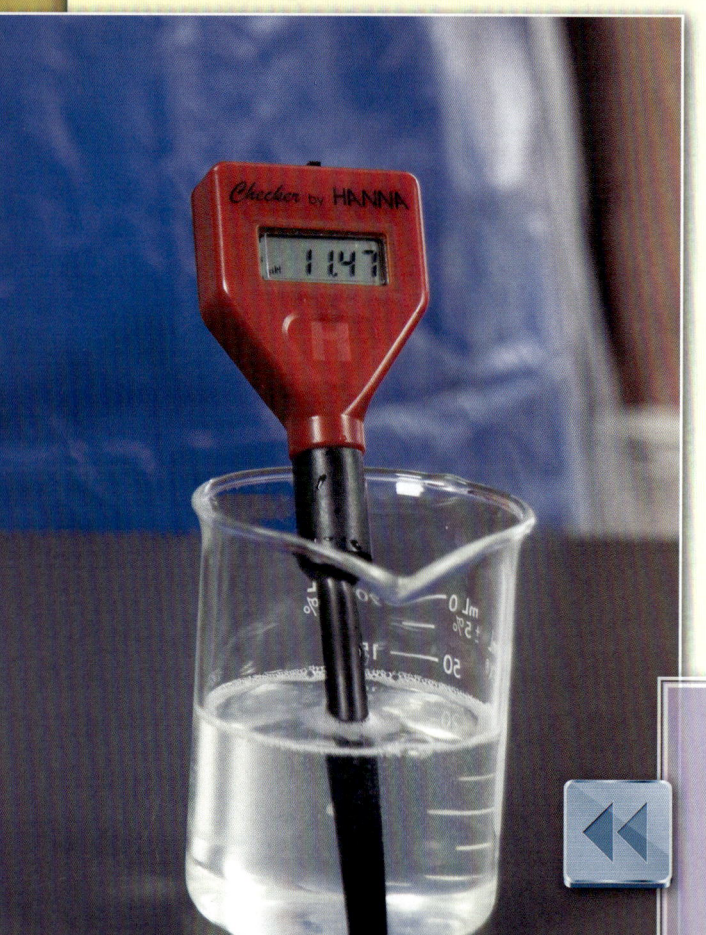

The word "calorie" has different meanings. One meaning refers to scientific measurements of heat and water. In science, a calorie is the amount of heat energy needed to raise the temperature of 1 gram (0.035 ounce) of water by 1 degree Celsius (1.8 degrees

This small device is called a calorimeter. It measures the amount of heat released from a liquid.

Wilbur O. Atwater was a chemist who lived a century ago. He developed a system to measure the caloric values of foods.

Fahrenheit). The more common meaning refers to the amount of energy contained in food. One food calorie is actually a "kilocalorie." It equals one thousand of the calories used in scientific measurements.

Compare and Contrast

Which form of exercise do you think burns more calories: rowing a boat or walking?

Calories and Weight

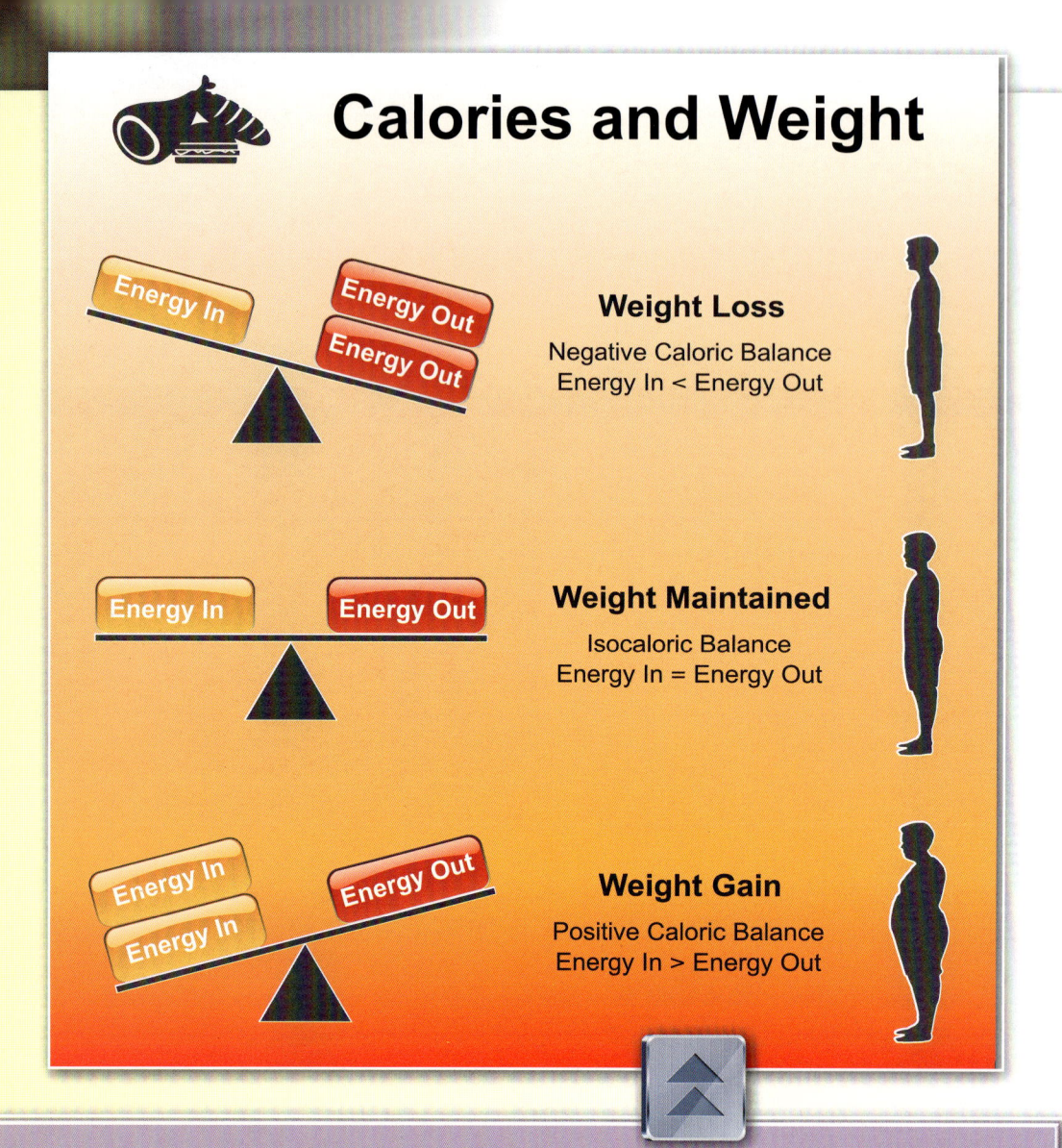

Weight Loss
Negative Caloric Balance
Energy In < Energy Out

Weight Maintained
Isocaloric Balance
Energy In = Energy Out

Weight Gain
Positive Caloric Balance
Energy In > Energy Out

This comparison chart shows that eating too many calories without getting enough exercise (*bottom*) adds weight.

8

> **VOCABULARY**
>
> **Nutrients** are things that the body needs to function and maintain itself. They are proteins, carbohydrates, fats, minerals, vitamins, and water.

Processed food manufacturers are required to state the number of calories contained in a package. This number is printed on the package label. Food manufacturers measure and add up the calories provided by each of the product's nutrients. The number of calories in each nutrient is determined by a scientific method known as the Atwater system.

Health scientists describe the calories that people consume in food as "energy in." The calories they burn during activities are "energy out." It is important for people to balance the amount of energy they take in with the amount of energy they burn.

How Many Calories Do People Need?

Some people need more calories than others. A person who sits at a computer all day does not burn as much energy as a carpenter who carries lumber, hammers nails, and saws boards.

The number of calories people need depends on many factors, including a person's gender, weight, height, and age. Most important, it depends on how active the person

People who work in offices, sitting at computers much of the day, burn few calories and need to get additional exercise.

is. The number may vary from day to day. A person who weighs 120 pounds (55 kilograms) may burn as many as 3,000 calories on a day when she is doing vigorous activities. If she spends most of the day reading and sleeping, she may use up about half that calorie count.

For a kid who weighs 60 pounds (27 kg), an hour of playing basketball can burn about 200 calories. An hour of doing homework can burn about 40 calories.

> **THINK ABOUT IT**
> What do you think height has to do with the number of calories a person needs?

Playing basketball for an hour burns 200–300 calories. The amount depends on the person's age, gender, and size.

Calorie Estimates for Children and Adults

The US National Library of Medicine provides the Estimated Energy Requirements (EER) table. It shows how many calories a person needs. The amount depends on the person's gender, age, and level of physical activity. Here are some examples.

An eight-year-old boy who is very active needs about 2,000 calories each day. An active

An eight-year-old boy who is moderately active needs about 1,600 calories every day.

> **COMPARE AND CONTRAST**
>
> Compared to others your age, do you think you are very active, not very active, or about average?

eight-year-old girl requires about 1,800 calories every day. If boys or girls of this age are inactive, they need only about 1,400 calories.

By the time a young person is sixteen, caloric needs increase greatly. An active boy at that age needs about 3,200 calories daily. An active girl and an inactive boy need about the same amount—2,400 calories. An inactive girl needs about 1,800 calories.

Most people require the highest levels of daily calories between their late teens and mid-thirties. On average, people older than seventy-five need only as many calories as children in their early teens.

These high school students get good calorie-burning exercise by participating in the marching band.

Calories Come with Carbohydrates

Carbohydrates, or carbs, are among nature's main sources of energy. They are **macronutrients**, or nutrients that people need in large amounts. Dieticians define two kinds of carbohydrates: simple and complex. All carbohydrates are made of molecules called sugars. Simple carbs are made up of one or two small molecules

Vocabulary

Macronutrients provide most of the energy contained in food. Macronutrients include carbohydrates, proteins, fats, and water.

White sugar, milk products, and many sweets and soft drinks contain simple carbohydrates.

> Complex carbs are found in food items such as bread, corn, potatoes, pasta, and grains like rice and barley.

of sugar. Complex carbs are made up of many large molecules of sugar. Every gram (0.035 ounce) of carbohydrates that a person eats adds four calories to the body.

A simple carbohydrate made up of one sugar molecule is called a monosaccharide. A simple carb made up of two sugar molecules joined together is called a disaccharide. Examples of simple carbohydrates are the sugars called glucose, fructose, and sucrose. Eating simple carbs raises the level of sugar in the bloodstream very quickly.

Complex carbohydrates are made up of many sugar molecules. Different patterns of these molecules form two types of nutrients: starches and fiber. Complex carbs raise the sugar level in the blood more slowly than simple carbs. Also, the sugar from complex carbs stays in the bloodstream longer. Dieticians think that calories from complex carbs are better for health than calories from simple carbs.

Calories in Sugar

Dieticians urge their patients to keep an eye on sugar intake. They are concerned about the amounts of sugar people eat. They also pay attention to the types of sugar their patients consume. Some forms of sugar are necessary. Others are less beneficial.

Dieticians think natural sugars are best for health. Natural sugars are those found in whole foods such as fruits and honey.

The healthiest forms of sugar are natural sugars. These children add honey, a popular natural sugar, to a cookie recipe.

COMPARE AND CONTRAST
Do you think table sugar is more or less beneficial than sugar contained in natural sources such as honey and apples?

Added sugars are the sugars found in processed foods. Food manufacturers add sugars to many foods to make them sweeter or tastier. Table sugar and corn syrup are common forms of added sugar. Popular soft drinks, candy, and ice cream contain added sugars.

Not all added sugars contain more calories than natural sugars. The reason added sugars are unhealthy is that they are unneeded. Many people fill up on sweetened foods and neglect foods that are healthier.

Soft drinks contain added sugars. Added sugars are used to create special flavors and are not necessary nutrients.

Calories in Fats

Fat is another kind of nutrient. Fat can be dangerous if it is out of control. But a certain amount of body fat is needed for good health. It produces and stores energy. Fat tissue helps keep the body warm. It cushions vital organs, pads the bones, and keeps the skin healthy. Fat is important for children's growth.

Fats in foods are also called fatty acids. There are several types, including unsaturated, saturated, and trans fats. All fats are high in calories, compared to other macronutrients.

Wise choices in a school cafeteria include vegetables and fruits and only small portions of fatty items.

Some brands of potato chips and doughnuts contain trans fats, which are especially unhealthy.

Vocabulary

The **circulatory system** is the maze of connected arteries and veins that move blood throughout the body.

One gram (0.035 ounce) of fat contains nine calories.

Unsaturated fats are found in oils and foods such as fish, nuts, and avocados. Saturated fats are found in red meats and dairy products. Trans fats can be found in packaged snacks such as candy bars, doughnuts, cookies, and potato chips.

Saturated fats and trans fats can be harmful. Over time, they can damage the heart and **circulatory system**. For that reason, dieticians recommend that people consume fewer saturated fats and trans fats.

Calories in Proteins

Proteins are chains of molecules called amino acids. Proteins are essential for growth and for repairing injuries. They keep muscles strong and bones sturdy. Every gram (0.035 ounce) of protein that people consume contains four calories—fewer than half the calories in a gram of fat.

Most humans obtain proteins by eating both animal and plant sources. Animal sources include meat, fish, poultry, dairy products, and eggs. These are called complete proteins because they contain all the amino acids the body needs. Plant sources include soy products, beans, seeds, and nuts. Different plant foods

Meat, fish, nuts, seeds, and dairy products are foods that are rich in proteins. Proteins help build muscles and bones.

To obtain enough proteins in their meals, vegans need to eat a variety of plant foods.

VEGAN SOURCES OF PROTEIN

- SOYBEANS
- QUINOA
- TOFU
- LEAFY GREENS
- CHICKPEAS
- BEANS
- MUSHROOMS
- BROCCOLI
- TEMPEH
- GREEN PEAS
- NUTS
- LENTILS
- CHIA SEEDS
- AVOCADO
- HEMP SEEDS
- BUCKWHEAT

contain different amino acids.

Vegans are people who eat no animal food products. They rely on plant sources for their proteins. No single plant source provides a complete store of amino acids. However, by eating a variety of plant foods, vegans can obtain the amino acids they need each day.

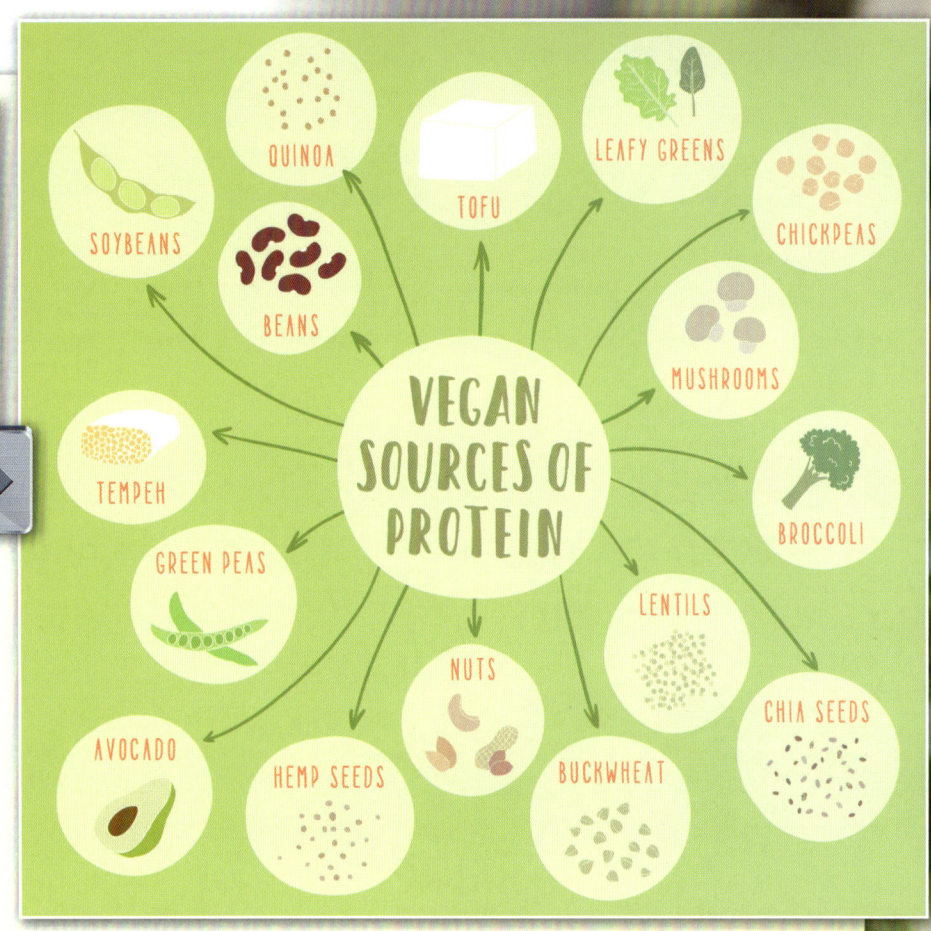

Think About It
What makes protein from animal sources different from plant protein?

Understanding Food Labels

The US Food and Drug Administration requires food producers to label their products with nutrition facts. This type of label contains information about a food item's nutritional values, including its calorie count. The calorie count is one of the first things most consumers look for.

A nutrition facts label also states how many servings of the product are inside the package.

In 2016, First Lady Michelle Obama explained the new nutrition facts label and its calorie information.

A girl studies the ingredients of a dairy product in a supermarket to learn about nutritional values.

An estimated **serving size** is determined by the food producer. The numbers on the label refer to the amount of each nutritional element contained in one serving.

When counting calories, a shopper must multiply the number of calories in a serving by the number of servings in the package. For example, a box of macaroni and cheese may show the number of calories as 250. If there are two servings in the box, then the box contains a total of 500 calories.

Vocabulary

A **serving size** is not an exact measurement. The serving size indicated on a nutrition facts label suggests the portion an average person will eat. In reality, one suggested serving may be enough to satisfy two or three children.

"Empty" Calories

Certain kinds of calories are particularly unhealthy. They are called "empty" calories. They are found in foods that are high in calories but low in beneficial nutrients. Examples are sweets, salty snacks, and soft drinks.

Millions of people have fallen into the habit of eating meals that contain empty calories. These include fast foods and packaged meals. They provide some

Snacking is OK if the snacks are healthy. Potato chips are not the healthiest choice.

Vocabulary

Packaged meals are complete meals that are sealed, often frozen, in one package. They require little or no serving preparation and may take only a few minutes to heat.

Packaged meals are quick to prepare and serve, but many of them provide too few nutrients.

vitamins, minerals, and other nutrients, but they lack others. They tend to contain high levels of sugar, salt, and unhealthy fats (saturated fats and trans fats).

A complete fast food meal may contain as many calories as some people need in a whole day. This type of meal fills the stomach and provides energy. It may provide some required nutrients. But it also adds unneeded calories that may be stored in the body as fat.

Problems Caused by Too Many Calories

A nurse takes a person's blood pressure. Reducing calories may help to lower high blood pressure.

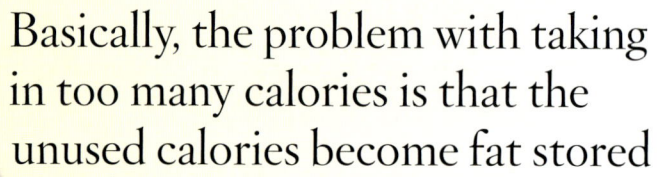

Basically, the problem with taking in too many calories is that the unused calories become fat stored inside people's bodies. A certain amount of stored fat is healthy. Over time, though, excess fat can create serious health problems. These problems often begin during childhood.

People who are overweight, especially those who are obese, have a higher risk of developing certain diseases. The risks increase if the person gets little physical exercise.

Some of these diseases can place the person's life in danger.

A doctor checks the blood sugar level of a boy who has diabetes. The most common type of diabetes is linked to obesity.

Vocabulary

Diabetes is a group of diseases that are related to the way the body uses blood sugar.

Diseases of the heart and circulatory system are serious concerns. Excess fat can damage blood vessels and force the heart to work harder. Diabetes, liver problems, and certain forms of cancer also are linked to excess weight.

Other weight-related diseases, such as arthritis, are not life-threatening. However, they can be painful and even disabling.

Balancing Calories and Activities

Doctors and dieticians try to help people keep a healthy weight. If an individual is underweight, a common recommendation is to take in more calories. If a person is overweight, health professionals advise eating fewer calories and getting more exercise.

It is not necessary for people to burn exactly as many calories as they consume every day. Instead, health professionals urge that everyone—young people and adults—adopt a smart lifestyle.

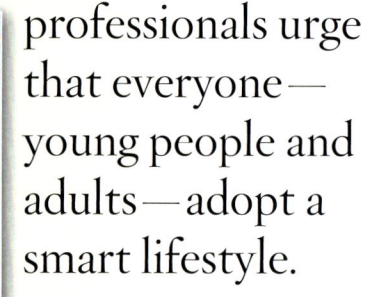

Swimming is an excellent form of exercise and fun. Daily exercise is vital for a healthy lifestyle.

Think About It

Start a personal plan for developing a healthy lifestyle. Think about the kinds of foods you should eat more or less of than others. Schedule exercise time each day. Ask a parent or teacher for suggestions to improve your lifestyle plan.

In addition to routine movements that burn energy, people should make time for daily exercise.

People also should educate themselves about food. They need to understand which items have good nutritional value and which ones are risky.

A father and daughter prepare a salad, a healthy, low-calorie dish. Kids should learn about wise food choices.

29

Glossary

artery One of the tube-shaped vessels that carry blood from the heart to all parts of the body.

arthritis A disease that causes a burning pain in the body's joints.

carbohydrates Substances found in certain foods, such as bread, rice, and potatoes, that provide the body with energy and are made of carbon, hydrogen, and oxygen.

complex Made up of many parts.

dietician A health professional who studies and advises people about their diets.

element One of the parts of which something is made.

energy Power that is contained in food and used for the body's activities.

fiber Material contained in food that helps the food move through the intestines.

gender A person's sex (for example, male or female).

molecule A particle, or tiny unit, of a substance.

obese Having an unhealthy amount of body fat.

processed Changed by special treatment, such as adding ingredients before being packaged and sold.

professional A person who does a job that needs special training, education, or skill.

proteins Substances that consist of chains of amino acids.

soy A class of foods made from soybeans and rich in protein.

starch A white carbohydrate found in potatoes, corn, wheat, and rice.

tissue A mass or layer of cells that form a structural material in the body.

vein One of the vessels that carry blood back to the heart from different parts of the body.

vigorous Done with great force and energy.

For More Information

Books

Are You What You Eat? A Guide to What's on Your Plate and Why! New York, NY: DK Publishing, 2015.

Bailey, Megan. *Healthy Eating Choices.* Mankato, MN: Child's World, 2014.

Dickmann, Nancy. *What You Need to Know About Obesity* (Fact Finders). North Mankato, MN: Capstone Press, 2016.

Hawley, Ella. *Exploring Food and Nutrition* (Let's Explore Life Science). New York, NY: PowerKids Press, 2013.

Lin, Grace, Ranida T. McKneally, and Grace Zong. *Our Food: A Healthy Serving of Science and Poems.* Watertown, MA: Charlesbridge, 2016.

Pelkki, Jane Sieving. *Healthy Eating* (A True Book). New York, NY: Children's Press/Scholastic Inc., 2017.

Ventura, Marne. *12 Tips for a Healthy Diet* (Healthy Living). Mankato, MN: 12-Story Library, 2017.

Websites

Choose My Plate
https://www.choosemyplate.gov
Facebook and Twitter: @MyPlate

GETFITTN
https://www.getfit.tn.gov/kids/calories.aspx

HealthHub
https://www.healthhub.sg/programmes/69/intro-to-calories

KidsHealth
http://kidshealth.org/en/kids/calorie.html
Twitter: @KidsHealth

Index

activity level, 10–11, 12, 13
age, 10, 12
amino acids, 20, 21
animal sources of protein, 20, 21
arthritis, 27
Atwater system, 9

burning calories, 5, 7, 9, 10, 11, 28, 29

calorie count, 22
calorie requirements, 10–11, 12–13
calories, what they are, 4–5, 6–7
carbohydrates, 9, 14–15
circulatory system, 19, 27
complete proteins, 20
complex carbohydrates, 15

diabetes, 27
disaccharide, 15

empty calories, 24–25

Estimated Energy Requirements table, 12
exercise, 29

fast food, 24, 25
fat, 5, 9, 14, 18–19, 25, 26, 27
fiber, 15

gender, 10, 12

heart, 19, 27
height, 10, 11

kilocalorie, 7

macronutrients, 14, 18
minerals, 9, 25
monosaccharide, 15

nutrients, 9, 14, 18, 25
nutrition labels, 22–23

obesity, 26

packaged meals, 24

plant sources of protein, 20, 21
processed food, 9, 17
proteins, 9, 14, 20–21

saturated fats, 18, 19, 25
serving size, 23
simple carbohydrates, 14, 15
starches, 15
sugar, 14, 15, 16–17, 25

trans fats, 18, 19, 25

unsaturated fats, 18, 19

vitamins, 9, 25

water, 9, 14
weight, and relation to calories required, 10
weight gain, 4, 5, 28
weight loss, 4, 5, 28